Tangled in Wisteria

J. Andrew Lockhart

Gotham Books

30 N Gould St.
Ste. 20820, Sheridan, WY 82801
https://gothambooksinc.com/

Phone: 1 (307) 464-7800

© 2024 *J. Andrew Lockhart*. All rights reserved.

No part of this book may be reproduced, stored in a retrieval system, or transmitted by any means without the written permission of the author.

Published by Gotham Books (December 20, 2024)

ISBN: 979-8-3305-8390-4 (H)
ISBN: 979-8-3304-1162-7 (P)
ISBN: 979-8-3304-1163-4 (E)

Because of the dynamic nature of the Internet, any web addresses or links contained in this book may have changed since publication and may no longer be valid.

The views expressed in this work are solely those of the author and do not necessarily reflect the views of the publisher, and the publisher hereby disclaims any responsibility for them.

Table of Contents

Praise for J. Andrew Lockhart v
Foreword vi
Acknowledgments vii
Introduction ix
Spring 1
Summer 25
Autumn 49
Winter 75
References 101
Backmattera 102

Praise for J. Andrew Lockhart

"Andy Lockhart is a living miracle. He overcame tremendous odds of surviving a brain hemorrhage and stroke at age 30 forcing him to give up a successful law practice and start over. In his "second life," Andy followed his heart to teach music and take up writing following the long road of physical and occupational therapy. The result of his journey is this collection of poems that will speak to the soul. From great pain and trial often comes great inspiration and depth. You will notice both in his work. I've known Andy and his devoted and gifted wife Toni for many years. I knew him when he was an up and coming attorney and as one who struggled to regain his speech, and now as a man reborn-spiritually, physically, and occupationally. The world can do without another lawyer, but we're better off because we've gained a poet and writer who will touch the souls of those who experience his art."

Mike Huckabee

Governor of Arkansas 1996-2007

Foreword

I first came across Andrew Lockhart's work on his poetry blog, Past Tense, and was immediately drawn in by his skilled verse. Adhering to the Japanese form of haiku and tanka, his poetry utilized deceptively simple features, such as a tanka composed of mostly one-syllable words that pack more of a punch than more ornate ones ever could. His pivots are dazzling, taking the reader from one juxtaposition to another quite seamlessly, without even realizing the shift is coming.

Mr. Lockhart's work explores a wide variety of layered themes, from loss, to life, from the mundane, to the magical, yet his mark of authorship clearly dwells upon each one. I know that I have enjoyed reading his poetry on a daily basis, and now invite you to thoughtfully and thoroughly delve into each verse as it appears on these pages. Come see how enriching the world of poetry-specifically the world of Andrew's poetry-can be.

Aurora Antonovic, *a recent Pushcart Prize nominee, is a Canadian writer, editor, and visual artist whose work has appeared over six thousand times in publications spanning twelve countries and five continents. She currently acts as haiga editor for Simply Haiku, and editor of A Little Archive of Poetry, a publication that seeks to promote verse in every form.*

Acknowledgments

Many thanks

to Grace Barlow and Jim Faught,

for teaching me the beauty of English

to Sarah Bates, Pat Bowles and Gerald Sloan,

for teaching me music

to Dr. Donna Gordy and Joyce Haver

for teaching me to teach

to Dr. Wendell Ross and Dr. Kent Sweatman,

for teaching me spiritually

to all of my family, especially Dad and Grandma,

for teaching me how to live

and most of all to Toni, my wife,

for teaching me how to love.

Introduction

June 14, 1996, after days of a horrible headache, became a day that would change my life forever. I had an intracerebral hemorrhagic stroke. The headache was caused by bleeding and rapid clotting in the frontal and temporal lobes on the left half of my brain. (We would later find out that the agent that tells the blood to clot was malfunctioning as well as the agent that tells blood to stop clotting). A craniotomy was performed the next night evacuating the hemorrhage, taking out brain tissue that had been damaged by the blood. Also, a ventriculostomy was used to drain the large amount of spinal fluid that continually built up pressure on my brain.

On June 17, the day after Father's Day, my heart stopped. This happened again in the next week. Hope for recovery was low, and by all means the story could have ended here.

Before the stroke I was an attorney and a partner with my father in a tax business. My son, James Andrew, Jr., had just turned one, and my wife and I were planning for another child.

I was thirty years old and had decided that this was the path that my life would take. What was missing, though, was an anchor for my soul to hold on.

At an early age there were two things that I truly loved-music and writing. I followed both of them to college. I majored in music education and spent much of my free time reading and writing. By my third year, though, doubt began to creep in. Instead of following my dream, I followed my pocketbook and went to law school.

I was a Christian, being baptized as a boy and understanding what that meant. The problem was that I never put that as number one on my list of importance. There was always something else taking its place, either work or personal matters.

Following the first week after the stroke, other problems began. Pneumonia set in and, due to the strong medicine, my kidneys began to shut down. I developed a clot in my leg, so I had a vent surgically placed to prevent a clot from making it to my lungs. The ventriculostomy, which was typically only to be used for about one week, was left for four weeks because the amount of spinal fluid around my brain kept rising. Finally, though, it was replaced by a shunt and I was moved to a regular hospital room.

I was then sent to the Baylor Rehabilitation Hospital in Dallas, Texas. The plan was to be there for six to eight weeks for intensive rehabilitation. After three weeks the shunt was clogged, so a new one was put in the right side of my head.

At that point the recovery moved faster than was planned. I was sent home after one more week. Riding into my driveway is the first memory I have of the whole ordeal.

It wasn't over, though. I spent the next few months at my office with my father. The days were spent on an easy-chair, being worked on by physical, occupational and speech therapists. By November I spent days at home with a therapist and by March, 1997, I was able to stay at home alone and was able to drive.

The next step was my vision. My right eye had been damaged due to the stroke and the shunt. I was having to wear an eye patch to keep from seeing double. After two surgeries on my eyes I was able to see with both eyes. I now wear glasses with a prism to allow me to see one image instead of two.

In 2000, thanks to a friend, I started working at a music store as an instrument repairman. Finally, a spot in the real world. Our second child, Katie, was born in April, 2001. By 2002, I was working as a part time Spanish teacher at the school where my wife taught. In 2003 I passed the state tests to become a certified music teacher. I made it.

After 22 years, I have fallen in love with teaching children. The Lord teaches me as I work with them. He has sent me two other children, too. Hannah was born in 2004 and John was born in 2006.

There was only one more step in my dream-writing. After years of relearning how to read and write I was drawn to poetry. I had written poetry years ago, but never was able to find the form that fit for me. That ended, though, when I ran into English version of the Japanese poems haiku and tanka.

Tanka, that were first called waka, began in Japan around the ninth century. They were written in five lines with 5-7-5-7-7 syllables. Their themes were personal and emotional, such as love, sadness or memories. Usually, the first three lines make a statement and the last two may go to another direction of the same theme.

In the seventeenth century, a new form of poetry grew from the tanka. This one, haiku, was made popular by the poet Basho (1644-94). Haiku are written in three lines in 5-7-5 syllables. Unlike tanka, haiku aren't based on emotion, rather on a specific moment of time in nature. Another form with the same structure is the senryu, which is usually humorous and isn't necessarily based on nature.

My knowledge of haiku was based only on elementary school exercises of counting syllables on three lines of 5-7-5. I found out, though, that to more keep the "feel" of Japanese poetry, the syllables weren't strict at all. English, structured so differently than Japanese, can make a haiku too cumbersome when one has to add words and rearrange lines to fit a 5-7-5 rule. The modern method, though, looks for the least amount of syllables rather than a specific amount of syllables. Tanka are treated the same way.

I write in both forms, capturing moments in everyday life. We don't know the amount, but the Lord has given us a certain amount of time here. Use them for all they are worth-year to year, season to season.

Spring

colors of spring

cover winter's carcass--

life after death

clouds glow from the full moon

at midnight--

his memories

awake the crickets

(1)

children's eyes

wandering out the window--

teaching in march

old gum

found by my fingers

under the chair--

you break my heart

again and again

(4)

Warmth

on my shoulder

her tears

she drives over

the mississippi river

as I listen--

left to sleep again

with the moon

dragonfly

skips over the brook--

shimmering sunset

(1)

cedar box,

fragrant and delicate,

holding her rose--

reminding me of

a day best forgotten

spring break--
children play baseball
while wearing coats

making the bed
listening to Bach,
St. Matthew Passion--
a child in the living room
plays chopstick on piano

toys left outside

in the heavy rain--

bathed in tears

the difference

between need and want

is lost

as robins fight

over a piece of bread

air full of the scent
of multicolor flowers--
funeral day

light rain
caresses the roof
at midnight--
she sighs
in a dream
(3)

on top

of an old pine tree

sits a crescent moon

hearing sounds

from many miles away

in the warm night

trying so hard to see you

in my mind's eye

one 7

another 95--

obituary

new limbs

growing from an old one,

cut short years ago--

just when you think

something's gone, it's back

pink tulips

above the daffodils--

watching the sunset

counting the stars

in a cloudy cool night

with my eyes closed--

slowly forgetting the sound

of your voice

spring is late--
looking at your
empty pillow

her words
in my cluttered mind
hang from wind chimes--
a distant thunder
forewarns the moon

night recital--

in the audience

a child yawns

(2)

holding hands

in the gallery

one by one

I see your face

on the wall

(5)

Wisteria

hangs on the gate

with lullabies

upon the fence

we see a butterfly

reminding us

of the days we jumped

rather than opening gates

hiding eggs

in the back yard--

stone rolls aside

afternoon,

hearing but not seeing

a woodpecker--

what will remind you

of me after I'm gone?

first warm night--
I hear a whippoorwill
in the field

paper airplane
swirls with leaves
in the wind
as chained dogs
demand freedom
(1)

walking barefoot--

navigating through

winter's remnant

writing alone

late at night-listening

to far away

traffic going west

and east

(2)

evening stroll--
sidewalk thick
with jasmine scent

American flag
moves by slowly through trees
by the river
laughter heard faintly
from the sand barge

inside an airplane
bonding with new friends
temporarily

half moon hangs
in the western sky--
walking in a field of wild flowers
looking for her name

a band-aid
cures the girl's sadness--
growing pains

perfume smell
of chamomile tea
opens my mind--
hearing her voice
in the flower garden

may afternoon-
flowers by the brook play
a watercolor fugue

I watch the river
as it meanders
to the east-
pulling barges
and memories

ninety degrees-

life gets longer

as spring gets shorter

flashing overhead

with thunder from the west

counting them all,

the nights we talked

until words were gone

late saturday night--
a far away car horn
plays dixie

(6)

looking up
at the oak tree, planted
when I was young--
there is no more need
for a mirror

Summer

crickets and frogs

loudly debate

under the stars

(6)

outside at night

drinking bottled water

deliberately

remembering my first

taste of white wine

watching the sky
I forget who I am—
soaring sunlight

noticing

a limb of an oak tree

has been cut down—

stealing the shade

for a moss covered tombstone

first feel of loss-
a boy's paper airplane
flies over a fence

although you are
so far away from me
I feel your presence
in the cool summer night
as flowers rest

evening walk-
fireflies dance
in the trees

she said
she would never
marry--
thinking of her while
watching my children
(3)

mockingbird
sings to the full moon-
summer night

the rain falls
into my dormant mind
as I sleep--
forgotten days walk
out of their secret room

the roof steams

from unexpected rain-

her perfume lingers

(1)

my blood pressure

rises while listening

to talk radio-

crickets peacefully talk

to the moon

june afternoon--
smell of fire fluid
and sounds of children

wives, husbands,
mothers, fathers and children
all seen together--
starting my day by reading
the obituaries

summer sunset--
leaving behind a wake
of wilted flowers

passion burns
as the breeze
blows through the fields-
watching her walk
through wild flowers

blue glass sky
shattered by the sun-
july morning

my daughter,
in her swimsuit,
looks out the window
watching robins splash
in the birdbath

(3)

hot concrete--
ants march fast
to the crack

the river,
slithering through
hot cracked ground,
follows the sun
that tells her sad story

crescent moon

smiling at the lake-

rippling mirror

walking close

on a dusty path

as the sun falls-

the bugs complain loudly

as if the heat is my fault

(3)

itchy legs--

mosquitoes congregate

by the pond

seeing you asleep

brings back feelings

of the day we met--

smell of honeysuckle

in the moon light

one strand left
of a spider web--
summer wind

tree shadows
the only thing moving
in the heat
sweat-soaked thoughts
slow in the heavy air

tombstone

visited only

by birds

walking through

a shop, I smell the scent

of your first perfume-

I smile and giggle

to a stranger

sadly watching

the last of sunlight-

summer solstice

I open my eyes

and see that it's now

july-

dressing for the heat, my mind

in new zealand winter

traveling

on a bottle rocket

to the half moon

your words follow

me through the day and

into the sunset-

I see one star after

another appear

buying a pack

of firecrackers

made in china

aimlessly walking

through downtown as a stranger,

watching strangers,

as my soul rests

at home far away

(3)

reflection,
the repetition of
summer sunlight

weeks
turn into months,
turning into years-
it's been too long
since I've seen you

late night breeze
through open windows-
honeysuckle thoughts

sitting on top
of the roof, watching
the sun sink
trying to resurrect
my childhood memories

dragonfly

skips over the brook-

shimmering sunset

looking west

as the sun falls

away-

followed by words,

leaving me empty

old man sits

at the picnic table-

misspelled graffiti

(6)

the tree,

having no chance to see

the rest of the world,

is told ancient stories

by the traveling moon

reading Job-
finding that my life
is not that bad

abandoned home
surrounded by
a wooden fence -- -
my spirit tangled in
unkempt wisteria

(3)

Autumn

my vision,

altered by fog

in the cool morning

sending the thoughts

from summer to fall

(3)

bare path--

looking up for the first

yellow leaf

heat tries hard

to divert my attention,

but it fails-

the sun falls earlier

today than yesterday

(3)

loud thunder-

political noise

from the radio

(7)

eyes closed,
mental liberty
fueled by the wind
bringing the first hint
of autumn

september morning
shadow under the oak
seems longer

downloading

Handel's Messiah

to an iPod--

hearing now the angels

while watching the stars

my mind

stretches beyond the earth-

day dream

introducing fall
in the play ground
under the clouds-
colorful piles of jackets
in the lost and found box

in my hand
a photo of you-
moon light

distant light

in another house

turns off-

looking to the west,

waiting for the sun

changing diapers-

longing for the sound

of the first flush

at sunset

I hear the bells

at the church,

finding myself alone

at your funeral... again

(4)

labor day walk-

light rain washes away

summer

this morning,

cooler than the one before,

warns me of the next-

envy fills me toward those

who now write about spring

(4)

sunset

falls through the moon-

october blue

my shoes

stacked in the closet

neatly-

arranging my future

step by step

listening to

79 rpm's

cobwebs in windows

(2)

afternoon rain

hammering on roofs

and trees-

children run wet,

smiling

park bench

covered with leaves

and thoughts

(1)

counting the hours
left of the day
as I collect my work,
noticing a "to do" list
from october... last year

autumn weekend-
leaves falling with
or without wind

above me,

falling from pine branches,

brown spent needles

on my unkempt hair-

thinner each autumn

(4)

kindergarten trip-

ducklings follow their mother

on the boardwalk

rising sun

climbs above the trees

and the roofs

as steam from the river

softens the brightness

tying my shoes-

feeling miles of walking

in my back

aftermath

of suicidal leaps

colorful leaves

soften my steps

from autumn to winter

a mouse

in the clutch of an owl-

full moon

raindrops bounce

off the shimmering

lake

as I walk alone,

missing my youth

(3)

global warming-

geography book left

by the window

last night

without you-

the magnitude

hits me as I see

the empty crib

trees weep

as a tombstone

tells a story

slowly walking

through a group of cedars

by the lake,

their age hidden by shade-

I try to do the same

hot air balloons

blend delicately with clouds-

watercolor dreams

children play

in the city park

under the sun

as the elderly man

walks with his oxygen tank

(3)

autumn weekend

sparkling sunlight shines

on bare limbs

monarch butterflies

disrupt my writing

of tanka-

flying away with them

in my autumn daydream

(4)

bad news

in the paper,

etc.

(7

ironing my shirt

slowly and clumsily,

thinking whether

I should be buried

in new clothes

(4)

handmade quilt

added to the bed-

mood swings

smoke rises
in a billowing cloud
then dissipations,
like thoughtless prayers
that deserve no answer

taking a day off--
hiding under dead leaves,
the ghosts of summer

falling in love

with the autumn leaves

watching them drop,

leaving me, yet again,

to face winter alone

trees whisper

to each other

at sunset

how can it be
spring in australia
if it's fall here?
she spins the globe
held upside down

(9)

windy
morning--
last leaf of the oak
floats to the ground

Winter

abandoned

by the sun

taking the warmth,

leaving me blind

to see tomorrow

sound of geese

flying away-

leaving us winter

thinking

of a crescent moon

while staring

at faceless clouds

as if they are mirrors

morning surprise--

her face appears suddenly

in my mind's eye

hardwood floor

cold to the feet

in the morning-

facing a day

and a past

(4)

coldfront-

watching you drive away

at sunset

antique shop

on main street-

shelter

from rain

and the present

(8)

winter warning-

electric blanket

defeats the alarm

thoughts
fall with snowflakes
to the ground-
leaving footprints
soon to disappear

brick after brick
after brick after brick-
hidden thoughts

the wind blows

beside the river

as always

your voice visits me

from far away

(4)

train sounds

interrupt my daydream-

her scent now distant

your song-

I hear it late at night

from a radio

left on

by accident

looking up--

tears hidden

by rain drops

campus bus
rolls into the night-
foreign man
leans over, saying
Merry Christmas

pirate ship
attacks the helpless yacht-
boy pulls the plug

the telephone is

our only connection

and barrier-

both outside

looking at the moon

(5)

his memories

ride the stream-

bruised by rocks

cold steady rain

attempts to wash

my sins,

unaware of the ones

that are hidden

the train bridge

allows dreams to pass

to mississippi

(2)

above the sky

stars silently watch

our lives-

no need of weather reports,

news updates or worries

ancient dust

lies still on the moon-

frozen time

off the roof
a loose shingle flies
in cold wind-
held back anger
finds it's first victim

to see the sun-
stretching above trees
and closing eyes

listening-

bad news after bad news

on the radio-

Amazing Grace bleeds in

from another station

(4)

moon hides behind

a cloudy quilt-

midnight shiver

spring-like weather
bathes the riverside,
geese dance in the air-
the radio tells me
"chance of snow on sunday"

one strand left
of a spider web-
winter wind

bare ground

partially covered

with yellow leaves

a coke bottle

reminds me of summer

(4)

syncopation-

downspout rattling

in winter rain

her ring

catches my eye

in the sunlight

as we walk, hand in hand

to her kindergarten

in the garden she

struggles with the ground-

rows of sadness

Chopin etude
at an art exhibition
as background
cold fingers create
their own form of beauty
(4)

afternoon walk-
holding hands in
heavy gloves

are they really

different from each other,

snow flakes,

landing on a newspaper,

life and death on one page

startling sounds

of steps on the roof-

faint bells

on the map
a moving line of white is
coming my way-
a loud skein of geese
ignores me as they pass

stars echo
in the hollow sky-
cold december

opening

a box of pastels,

looking

for colors that bring back

the feeling of spring

looking up-

the moon hangs in a shroud

of my breath

way too cold
to be outside, but don't tell
the mockingbird-
hearing his song
long before sunrise

second half
of the year's last game--
winter solstice

in the morning air

I'm able to see

my breath

for just a moment-

nothing is permanent

march first-

dusty short sleeve shirts

unboxed

(2)

Unsuccessfully
trying to pronounce the names
on the pill bottles-
what happened to days
when aspirin was enough?

old man laughs-
winter slowly melts
into spring

References

Several poems included in Tangled in Wisteria were originally printed in various journals and collections. They are reprinted here with permission courtesy of the editors of:

(1) Stylus Poetry Journal (Dec. 2005)

(2) Haiku Harvest (Vol. 6, No. 1)

(3) Modern English Tanka (Vol. 1 No. 1)

(4) Modern English Tanka (Vol. 1 No. 2)

(5) Fire Pearls-edited by M. Kei

(6) clouds peak (Issue 1, July 2006)

(7) clouds peak (Issue 2, October 2006)

(8) American Tanka (Issue 16)

(9) Eucalypt (Issue 1)

Backmatter

In real life, can tragedy truly turn into triumph? Absolutely! J. Andrew Lockhart tells us in Tangled in Wisteria how this happened in his life. This story of his amazing victory is followed by a collection of his modern English versions of the Japanese poems of tanka, haiku and senryu. Movingly written, these short poems reveal the beauty of the seasons of nature and of life.

"Andy Lockhart is a living miracle. The result of his journey is this collection of poems that will speak to the soul. From great pain and trial often comes great inspiration and depth. You will notice both in his work. [W]e're better off because we've gained a poet and writer who will touch the souls of those who experience his art."

Mike Huckabee

Governor of Arkansas 1996-2007

J. Andrew Lockhart was once an attorney, but now is a poet and a retired elementary music teacher. His work has been published in three countries in books and journals, such as Modern English Tanka, American Tanka, Haiku Harvest, Fire Pearls and Eucalypt. Also, some of his poetry has been translated into Japanese, Russian, and Finnish. He lives in Van Buren, Arkansas with his wife, Toni, and has four children, James (and daughter-in-law Alahna), Katie, Hannah, and John.

www.ingramcontent.com/pod-product-compliance
Lightning Source LLC
LaVergne TN
LVHW012247070526
838201LV00090B/147